RETURNING TO LEARNING

Getting Your GED

Rick Conlow

A Step-by-step Formula for
Future Success and Opportunity

CRISP PUBLICATIONS, INC.
Los Altos, California

RETURNING TO LEARNING
Getting Your GED

Rick Conlow

CREDITS
Editors: **W. Philip Gerould and Anne Knight**
Designer: **Carol Harris**
Typesetting: **Interface Studio**
Cover Design: **Carol Harris**
Artwork: **Ralph Mapson**

Copyright © 1990 by Crisp Publications, Inc.
Printed in the United States of America

Crisp books are distributed in Canada by Reid Publishing, Ltd., P.O. Box 7267, Oakville, Ontario, Canada L6J 6L6.

In Australia by Career Builders, P.O. Box 1051, Springwood, Brisbane, Queensland, Australia 4127.

And in New Zealand by Career Builders, P.O. Box 571, Manurewa, New Zealand.

Library of Congress Catalog Card Number 89-81521
Conlow, Rick
Returning To Learning
ISBN 1-56052-002-7

PREFACE

You may miss out on thousands of dollars a year in possible income if you lack one key element to success: a high school education. With a high school diploma or its equivalent, doors to jobs or a college education will swing open for you. But without that diploma, your future remains severely limited.

This book has been designed for people who need a high school diploma and who want one—but who don't want to return to school to get it. You may be eighteen, twenty-eight, forty-eight, or sixty-eight; it doesn't really matter. If you make up your mind to get the high school equivalency diploma (GED), you *can* get it—and you don't have to return to school. RETURNING TO LEARNING: Getting Your GED, outlines a formula that assures you success.

You will need other resources, but this book serves as your key starting point. Read through it, pencil in hand, and when you finish you should be prepared to pass your GED exam.

Did you know that most people fail to get the GED because:

- They don't know about the GED or how to get it.
- They fear failure, and they lack the self-confidence to try.
- They don't know how to prepare to take the GED tests.
- They lack a plan to succeed.

The formula described in RETURNING TO LEARNING will help you overcome the obstacles just mentioned above. You'll understand exactly what is needed for you to achieve your goal. By reading this book, you'll learn about:

- The 5 tests on the GED exam
- 7 surefire ways the GED will help you
- 13 powerful ways to build the self-confidence to succeed
- 3 primary methods of studying for the GED
- 33 secret test-taking tips
- 11 additional resources to get help with the GED
- 3 important things to do after you get your GED

Ready to begin? May the best of luck be yours!

Rick Conlow

CONTENTS

CONTENTS (Continued)

INTRODUCTION

WHAT IS THE GED?

The letters GED stand for General Educational Development. The GED is a federal program designed for adults (usually 18 or older) who have not completed high school. Approximately one million people drop out of school every year, so if you don't have a high school diploma, you are not alone. Most people who leave school early don't want to return, especially if it's been years since they left. The GED provides a way for people without a high school diploma to document their educational attainment. The GED also provides a passport to a better future.

The GED Testing Service, American Council on Education, in Washington, D.C., administers the program, while local organizations, colleges, or programs sponsor the tests. Anyone is eligible to take the tests who is not currently enrolled in high school, or has not graduated from high school. Other requirements are sometimes also set by individual states, territories, or provinces, with regard to age, the length of time since you left school, and residency. More information on this is given later in the book.

The GED tests determine a person's level of educational development in these areas: writing skills, social studies, science, literature and the arts, and mathematics. The questions in each test are geared toward general knowledge and ideas, and a person's ability to think critically. Few questions require knowledge of specific facts, dates, details, or information. Anyone who can solve and deal with everyday experiences, will probably do well on the GED tests.

If you're reading this book because you dropped out of school, be clear on this point:

> **You're not a failure because you didn't finish high school!**

People drop out of school for many reasons, and not finishing doesn't mean you're a loser. You can't undo the past, but you can move forward. Keep this in mind: each year about 400,000 people pass the GED tests. **You can too—if you want to.** If you follow the formula for success described in the next few pages, you'll soon have your GED certificate, too.

WHY YOU LEFT HIGH SCHOOL

CHECK ALL THAT APPLY ☑

- ☐ 1. You wanted to get a job.
- ☐ 2. You wanted to get married.
- ☐ 3. You were going to have a baby.
- ☐ 4. You moved and didn't like the new school.
- ☐ 5. You needed to earn money to help provide for your family.
- ☐ 6. You were bored.
- ☐ 7. You weren't interested.
- ☐ 8. You had poor grades.
- ☐ 9. You had personal problems.
- ☐ 10. You got into trouble.
- ☐ 11. You felt school was too hard.
- ☐ 12. You felt school was too easy.
- ☐ 13. You didn't like school.
- ☐ 14. Your parents made you quit.
- ☐ 15. Other: _____

People usually cite one or more of the reasons listed above as why they left school. Whatever your reason, now is the time to put it behind you. Think instead of what's ahead of you: What do you really want out of life?

All of these are excellent reasons for moving ahead—and one of the best ways to move ahead is to get the credentials that show you're qualified for something better. The credential you need first of all is the GED.

IMPORTANT

Most GED tests consist of multiple choice questions in which five possible answers are given. The questions cover a broad range of topics. Some questions are easy; some are harder.

Part II of the Writing Skills Test is not multiple choice. For this test, you write an essay on what you believe about a certain topic.

The tests are timed and you are allowed a maximum of 7½ hours to complete them. In some places, you must take all the tests on the same day; in others, you can take tests on different days.

Check out the requirements in your area before you test and find out if you need an appointment to test. (More suggestions follow later in the book.)

THE WRITING SKILLS TEST

Part I of the Writing Skills Test covers spelling, punctuation, capitalization, grammar, and arranging sentences in a logical order. The test does not use words beyond the ordinary high school student's vocabulary. The test has 55 questions, divided as follows:

30%—spelling, punctuation, capitalization
35%—usage and grammar
35%—sentence structure

SAMPLE QUESTION

(Shade in the best answer)   Which of the following words is misspelled:

a   b   c   d   e   a. height

0   0   0   0   0   b. coperate

c. weight

d. commitment

e. canoeing

(Answer: b. Cooperate is the correct spelling.)

Part II of the Writing Skills Test is an essay. You will be asked to write about a broad topic such as:

• violence on TV
• religion in schools
• nuclear disarmament

Include in your essay information what *you* think should be done about the topic you choose, or how *you* would handle the situation. The test examiner will score you on how you organized your thoughts, your spelling, and grammar, and whether or not what you have written makes sense. The test takes 45 minutes.

A sample Writing Skills Test is included later in this book.

THE SOCIAL STUDIES TEST

The Social Studies Test covers history, economics, political science, geography, and behavioral sciences. **You do not need to memorize facts, dates, or figures.** You will need to know general information about each area. The test examines your ability to read social studies passages and interpret and draw conclusions about what you read. The time allowed for the test is 85 minutes. It has 64 questions, divided as follows:

25%—history
20%—economics
20%—political science
15%—geography (20% in Canada)
20%—behavioral sciences (15% in Canada)

SAMPLE PASSAGE AND QUESTION

The Supreme Court ruled in the *Miranda* case that police must tell a prisoner what his rights are. In the *Escobedo* decision police power is limited in searching for evidence in a person's house.

(Shade in the best answer)

Let's say the police wanted to search for evidence in your home. What would they probably have to do?

a b c d e

0 0 0 0 0

a. Ask your neighbor for help.

b. Contact a lawyer for a ruling.

c. Enter your house while you were away if they suspected something.

d. Send a SWAT team to break into your house when you're not home.

e. Get special permission from a judge.

(Choice [e] is the best answer, because the passage states that police powers are limited in searching people's homes.)

THE SCIENCE TEST

The Science Test deals with two major areas: life sciences and physical sciences. Once again, **you will not need to memorize facts, formulas, or scientific terms.** You will need to have an understanding of fundamental ideas in biology, earth science, chemistry, and physics.

The test examines your ability to read passages in science and to interpret and draw conclusions from what you read. Reading material is taken from modern newspapers, magazines, journals, and textbooks. The time allowed for the test is 95 minutes. There are 66 questions, divided as follows:

50%—life sciences
50%—physical sciences

SAMPLE PASSAGE AND QUESTION

An organ in a living thing is a group of tissues that carry on a specific function. Leaves, hearts, brains, and lungs are examples of organs.

(Shade in the
best answer)   Which of the following is not an organ:

a   b   c   d   e   a. liver

0   0   0   0   0   b. stems

c. biceps

d. eyes

e. none of the above

(The best answer is [c]. Biceps aren't an organ; they're the name of a specific muscle group. Stems are an organ in a tree.)

LITERATURE AND THE ARTS TEST

Reading is important for the Literature and the Arts Test. You will be asked to read several passages and answer multiple choice questions about them. You will be required to identify the main idea of the reading, draw conclusions about the information, follow directions, understand humor, and recognize major ideas.

Reading passages are taken from many kinds of literature related to everyday types of reading—magazines, newspaper articles, recipes, library references, advertisements, political cartoons, instructions, and contracts. Allowed time for the test is 65 minutes. It includes 45 questions, divided as follows:

50%—popular literature
25%—classical literature
25%—commentary on Literature and the Arts

SAMPLE PASSAGE AND QUESTION

Sales is an excellent career opportunity. It's been called the lowest paid easy work and the highest paid hard work. There are thousands of people selling many kinds of products who do just enough to get by and who don't make much money. On the other hand, some salespeople apply themselves by receiving proper training, setting goals, taking care of customers, and working long hours—and they build a big income.

(Shade in the best answer)

A good title for the passage is:

a b c d e   a. Super Star Salespeople

0 0 0 0 0   b. It's Easy to Fail in Sales

                    c. Work Hard and Succeed in Sales

                    d. Successful Sales Involves Luck

                    e. None of the above

(The best answer is [c], because hard work is described as the key to success in sales.)

A sample Reading Test is included later in this book.

THE MATHEMATICS TEST

The Mathematics Test focuses on basic arithmetic, but it includes some algebra and geometry as well. If you can do fractions, decimals, and percentages you will be able to do well on this test. All questions are in word problem format. In other words, you will read about a problem and be instructed to answer questions related to it.

Time allowed for the test is 90 minutes. It has 56 questions, divided as follows:

50%—arithmetic
30%—algebra
20%—geometry

SAMPLE WORD PROBLEM

(Shade in the best answer)	You found a shirt you liked at the store. Its price tag indicated that it cost $15.00, but all store merchandise was on sale that day at 10% off. How much did you pay for it?
a b c d e	a. $16.50
0 0 0 0 0	b. $12.00
	c. $14.90
	d. $13.50
	e. $13.05

(The correct answer is [d]. 10% of $15.00 is $1.50, and $15.00 minus $1.50 [the sale discount] equals $13.50.)

A sample test is included later in this book.

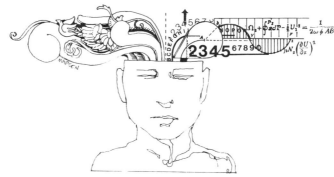

A SAMPLE GED TEST RESULT

SCORING IS DIFFERENT FROM HIGH SCHOOL

The score you receive on the GED test is very different from what you may remember from high school. The score you receive is called a "standardized score."

There are two important standardized scores to remember. A score of **35** or above means that you passed an individual test. (In some states a passing grade is 40 or above.) After you take all five tests, the five scores are averaged. This average must be **45** or above to pass. Being strong in one area can help make up for being weak in another area. An average score of 45 or above will earn you your GED certificate. To get this score, you will need to have at least 225 points from correct answers, which means answering about half the questions on each test correctly.

Example:

Test	Score
1. Writing Skills	44
2. Social Studies	49
3. Science	50
4. Literature	52
5. Mathematics	35

$$\text{Average} \quad \frac{230}{5} = 46$$

These scores mean that the student has passed each individual test, since all scores are 35 or above. The average score of 46 entitles the student to a GED certificate.

A FORMULA FOR SUCCESS

STEP 1: KNOW WHAT THE GED MEANS TO YOU

STEP 2: BUILD YOUR CONFIDENCE TO SUCCEED

STEP 3: DETERMINE WHAT YOU NEED TO STUDY

STEP 4: MAKE A PLAN TO ACHIEVE YOUR GOAL

The Four Steps above constitute a Formula for Success in earning your GED certificate. Hundreds of people have followed these four steps to win their GED high school equivalency certificates. Over 98% of the people who worked through each step successfully completed the GED tests.

The next four sections of the book describe each of the four steps. **Don't skip a step.** Follow the Formula for Success exactly. The steps will show you—step-by-step—how to be successful.

Now, get started, and don't quit!

STEP 1 | KNOW WHAT THE GED MEANS TO YOU

BENEFITS OF THE GED

Getting your GED is a worthy goal and an important step in furthering your education. In the last five years, about 2 million people have received GED's.

The GED is accepted by nine out of 10 businesses and colleges in place of a high school diploma. Sometimes, having a GED can even provide an advantage, because having completed it shows initiative and determination to get ahead.

Studies indicate that nearly one-third of today's high school graduates would fail the GED tests. So, possessing your GED should indicate to potential employers or college admissions officers that your academic achievment is better than almost one-third of those students who graduate from high school.

Here are some benefits of receiving the GED. Check all that apply for you.

_____ 1. You will be eligible for many more jobs. (About 92% of today's jobs require a high school diploma or its equivalent.)

_____ 2. You will achieve an important goal and feel good about yourself.

_____ 3. You will receive more job promotions, because you'll be a more qualified employee.

_____ 4. You will receive a high school equivalency certificate (diploma) from your state's Department of Education.

_____ 5. You will improve your basic skills (reading, math, English) through diligent practice and study and be better able to handle everyday activities.

_____ 6. You will be able to enter any community college and most major colleges of your choice to further your education.

_____ 7. You will be able to enter any technical or vocational program that meets your needs for additional training.

HOW THE GED HELPS YOU MEET YOUR NEEDS

You want the GED because you know that it will help you meet your needs. You may need to earn more money for a variety of reasons. You may need a better-paying job but can't get one without a high school diploma. You may need to write or to read better to get a job promotion. Or, you may want to get along better in everyday life. You need to do something different to feel good about yourself. You may need to meet new people and make new friends. In other words, you want more out of life than you're getting. The GED can unlock the doors to many opportunities.

Having the GED won't solve all of your problems, but once you have it, you will find that you're getting more out of life.

Why do **you** want the GED? In the space below, write why you need the GED. Be as specific as possible.

Obstacles can stand in the way of your getting the GED: Peer pressure, lack of time, work, weariness, laziness, doubt, fear, and criticism. *Every time you face an obstacle, reread what you just wrote above. It will remind you of what you have to gain if you persevere—and what you will lose out on if you don't!*

YOU DESERVE IT, DON'T YOU?

Do you deserve the best out of life? Do you deserve to earn more money, get a higher-paying job, receive a promotion, or be happy?

Some people have a difficult time answering "yes" to those questions. They may be letting past mistakes make them feel unworthy or undeserving of the good things in life. They feel like failures. They may feel that they can't get the GED because:

- ☐ They're too old.
- ☐ They're too young.
- ☐ They're not smart enough.
- ☐ It's too late for them.
- ☐ They feel they're not important.
- ☐ They say they can't do it.
- ☐ They don't know how.
- ☐ It's too hard.
- ☐ What if they fail?

If you've had any of these thoughts, place a check mark ☑ in the space provided. Be aware that these thoughts will cause you to settle for less. These thoughts can keep you from getting the GED.

The fact is, **YOU *DO* DESERVE THE BEST OUT OF LIFE!** You are a unique person with your own special qualities and talents. You have much to offer yourself and others. But it's your choice and responsibility to make it happen. It will take a plan, hard work, and determined effort to succeed!

DO YOU DESERVE THESE?

Circle (yes) for each area that applies to you.

   1. I'd like to get a better job.   YES

   2. I'd like to move ahead in life.   YES

   3. I'd like to develop more self-confidence.   YES

   4. I'd like to prepare for a better future.   YES

   5. I'd like to feel good about myself.   YES

   6. I'd like to develop more self-discipline.   YES

   7. I'd like to understand myself better.   YES

   8. I'd like to continue my education.   YES

   9. I'd like to accomplish my goals.   YES

 10. I'd like to be recognized for an achievement.   YES

 11. I'd like to gain the admiration of others.   YES

 12. I'd like to get into the armed services.   YES

 13. I'd like to advance in a job.   YES

 14. I'd like to earn more money.   YES

 15. I'd like to set a positive example for others.   YES

 16. I'd like to overcome past obstacles or mistakes.   YES

Furthering your education by getting your GED can help you achieve any or all of your goals.

> "People were born to succeed, not fail."—*Henry David Thoreau*

GETTING STARTED

A sixth-grade boy was having difficulties in school, but he figured once he got into junior high, life would be great. In junior high, though, school wasn't any better: he was teased because his voice was changing, and he consistently received poor grades.

Once he got out of school, he thought life would be better. School finally ended, and he went on to work. But life still didn't improve much for him. Being married was fine for a time, but marriage eventually didn't turn out the way he wanted, either.

Then he decided that once he retired, he could do what he wanted and be what he wanted to be. Life would be great! The day finally came. As he sat in his favorite chair, his thoughts wandered back on what it was like to be young, in the sixth grade again. The memories brought tears to his eyes, when he realized he'd missed the opportunities to be what he wanted to be. The years had passed so quickly and he'd never really lived. He was always so worried or anxious for the future that he'd never lived for today.

What do **you** want out of life? Take a lesson from this little story and get started on the life you want **today.** Don't wait for tomorrow. Live life fully **today.** Life isn't a dress rehearsal or trial run for the future, so don't put off what's important. If the GED certificate is important to you, then get it!

It will take determined effort—anywhere from a few days of study to several months, depending on your situation. A survey of 100 people studying for the GED certificate reported that it took them an average of 37½ hours to review for the tests. That means that most people can spend a few hours a week studying. (This book will explain how to study in a later chapter.)

Have you ever wanted to do a project but just never got started? Have you ever started something and never finished it? You'll avoid falling into either of these traps on your road to the GED if you keep in mind the benefits you'll receive (see page 11), and if you keep reminding yourself of your goal. Step 4 of Your Formula to Success will show you how to develop a goal that you can achieve.

Having a goal will get you started. Once you get started, gaining confidence and maintaining discipline will help you achieve it.

> **You do want the GED, don't you?**
> **You do deserve the GED, right?**

Then, move on to the next step. Don't skip ahead because you'll miss an important ingredient to your success—gaining self-confidence!

SUCCESS STORY #1:
JIM'S BUSINESS

Jim dropped out of high school one year before graduation. It wasn't that he was failing in school; he had good grades. But school bored him. He was eager to get out into the world, to get a job and earn his own way.

He soon found that the best jobs he could get were working at gas stations for little over minimum wage. In a couple of years, he'd had enough of low-paying jobs and decided he'd better get his high school diploma. So he began to study on his own for the GED, stressing work on math and reading.

It didn't take long. Within a few short weeks, he felt confident that he could pass all the GED tests—and he did! Jim had the ability to do well; having the GED boosted his belief in what he could do.

Shortly after Jim got his GED, he started his own janitorial service. He had enough confidence to call on business owners and sell his services. Now, at age 20, he's on his way to more success. Next he plans to enter college part time to earn a business degree.

STEP 2 | BUILD YOUR CONFIDENCE TO SUCCEED

The reason that many people don't go after their GED is because they lack self-confidence. They don't believe in themselves, because they've felt like failures for some time. They are afraid of making mistakes, and when the going gets tough, they simply give up.

You may feel the same way. You may believe that other people feel that you won't succeed—at anything! You may not even be sure yourself whether you can.

Don't worry about having these thoughts—it's **normal** to have some doubts, to be nervous, and to question your ability and determination.

But when you begin doubting yourself, stop and think of areas where you have succeeded. You know that you can finish something you really want to. Maybe you've raised a family, solved problems, fixed up a home, finished a class, built something, planned a trip, helped a friend, or organized a group. Any such actions prove that you can succeed at what you tackle. You do have abilities. Now think about this: The same personal traits that helped you achieve all these other projects are the same ones you need to get your GED.

The following pages contain some exercises that are designed to make you feel more self-confident.

EXERCISES AHEAD

EXERCISE 1: LIFE STATEMENTS

See yourself as being confident and positive, and you'll begin to live your life that way. It's this simple: Continued positive thoughts produce positive results, and negative thoughts yield negative results. Think of positive things now and fill in the blanks to each of the following statements:

1. I like to _____

2. I really enjoy _____

3. I dream about _____

4. I look forward to _____

5. I'm a good friend because _____

   _____

6. One thing I've always wanted to do is _____

   _____

7. Something I've recently learned is _____

8. I feel good when _____

9. I think it's funny when _____

   _____

10. I get excited about _____

11. One thing I'm proud of is _____

12. One thing I do well is _____

13. What I want people to remember about me is _____

14. I'm happiest when _____

15. My best quality is _____

Now read over your list. Feel pretty good about yourself, don't you? When you stop to think about it, you're quite a person!

EXERCISE 2: PERSONAL SUCCESS

What is success? It is most often defined in terms of wealth, influence, and power. But there's a better way to define it. Success is doing something the way you want to do it. It's a state of being, of feeling good about yourself and others, regardless of the circumstances in which you live.

People usually feel that if they don't have a lot of money, education, or social influence, they aren't successful. **Don't buy into that view.** It destroys your self-confidence, and may cause you to stop trying to reach your goals or improve your situation.

This is how Ralph Waldo Emerson defined success:

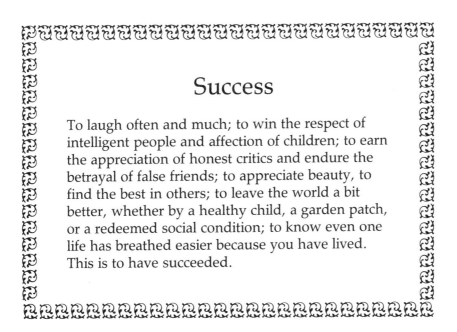

Success

To laugh often and much; to win the respect of intelligent people and affection of children; to earn the appreciation of honest critics and endure the betrayal of false friends; to appreciate beauty, to find the best in others; to leave the world a bit better, whether by a healthy child, a garden patch, or a redeemed social condition; to know even one life has breathed easier because you have lived. This is to have succeeded.

PERSONAL SUCCESS

How many times have you been successful? A few times? The truth is, it's probably been hundreds of times. You just tend to remember your failures more than your successes. Take time to list your successes below. Include such experiences as fixing a car, helping someone in need, raising your children, working two jobs, or volunteering to help a charity. Give yourself some credit and a pat on the back. List things you do well or have done well in the past.

1._____

2._____

3._____

4._____

5._____

6._____

7._____

8._____

9._____

10._____

11._____

12._____

13._____

14._____

15._____

IMPORTANT

Fill in *all* 15 spaces. Review the list often. It'll remind you that you have accomplished a lot already, and that you can achieve even more, including getting your GED! When things aren't going well, reread this success list. It'll spur your confidence and remind you that you're a winner, not a loser.

EXERCISE 3: POSITIVE CHARACTERISTICS

Everyone has strengths or positive characteristics. However, it may seem that other people like to point out what's wrong with us. Do you ever remember someone asking you if you would ever amount to anything? When asked to list their strengths and weaknesses, studies reveal that most people list three times as many weaknesses.

People tend to take their strengths for granted. Strengths come in many forms. For example, being enthusiastic, being a good listener, and acting in thoughtful, kind, and courteous ways are all positive characteristics. People don't want to be boastful, but if they minimize their strengths and maximize their weaknesses, their self-confidence will surely suffer. Beware of this trap; it'll keep you from creating a better life by continuing your education.

In this exercise, emphasize your strengths. For once, don't worry about bragging. Recognize your abilities and talents, and count them as assets.

"MY STRENGTHS INCLUDE:"

POSITIVE CHARACTERISTICS

Check all that describe you.

1. Caring attitude	_____	16. Intelligent	_____
2. Hard-working	_____	17. Kind	_____
3. Honest	_____	18. Good listener	_____
4. Logical	_____	19. Thoughtful	_____
5. Competitive	_____	20. Determined	_____
6. Ambitious	_____	21. Positive	_____
7. Enthusiastic	_____	22. Healthy	_____
8. Goal-oriented	_____	23. Intuitive	_____
9. Loyal	_____	24. Happy	_____
10. Creative	_____	25. Confident	_____
11. Good communication skills	_____	26. Imaginative	_____
12. Persistent	_____	27. Analytical	_____
13. Sense of humor	_____	28. Assertive	_____
14. Patient	_____	29. Other: _____	
15. Spiritual	_____	30. Other: _____	

Add any other positive characteristics you possess that aren't listed above. Don't be bashful about your good points. This exercise is for your use only. Let the positive traits fuel your inner confidences as dry wood does a fire.

SUCCESS STORY #2:
THERESA'S AMBITION

Theresa had a bad start in life. Her home situation was poor, and her parents repeatedly belittled most of her efforts. To escape from this environment, she left school before graduation, intending to make a better life on her own.

It wasn't easy. Since she had no high school diploma, the only jobs available to her were very low-paying, and she often found she wasn't treated much better than she had been at home.

What could she do? She realized that the first step was to get her high school diploma. Since she was in her 20s and didn't want to return to high school, she enrolled in a GED program. The program leader recognized that Theresa was bright, and helped Theresa realize it herself.

All Theresa needed was a shot of self-confidence, a belief that she was able to do well. She passed the GED tests easily and received her GED certificate. With her new-found self-confidence and GED in hand, Theresa landed a job as assistant manager in a fast-food restaurant. She quickly moved on to become the manager. Later, she enrolled in college to take business classes. Her next goal is to get a college degree.

TEN CONFIDENCE BOOSTERS

1. **Like yourself.** Know in your heart that you're a good person. It's difficult to have confidence in someone you don't like. Begin today not to criticize yourself. In fact, try not criticizing others. At the end of each day, review what you did well.

2. **Believe in yourself.** Believe that you can do many things. First, you believe, then things happen.

3. **Enjoy life.** Have fun. Seek out the little things in life, too. If you make a mistake, laugh at it, but learn from it. Play with a child. Watch a sunset. Smell the roses. Reward yourself for studying an hour. Celebrate with friends when you get the GED.

4. **Take action.** You'll feel good about yourself when you do something positive. Make an honest effort. Try something. Always take the first step even if it's a little one.

5. **Listen to good music.** Studies show that music affects people positively. Listen to music that is pleasing and comfortable. Use music to build you up, not to depress you.

6. **Be with positive people.** Visit and talk with people who help you. Don't hang around with people who tear you down. Be with people who support you and make you feel good about yourself.

7. **Help others.** It seems to work out that if you help others succeed, you succeed. And helping also helps you gain self-confidence.

8. **Take a risk.** It's exciting to try something new, to take a chance. You grow as a person. You gain a positive outlook on life. There is a saying "you have to be willing to look bad before you can look good."

9. **Keep learning.** In all situations, learn something. Then **all** situations—no matter how bad—can still be useful. If you make a mistake, learn from it. Be willing to admit it when you don't know, or when you need help. Read as much as you can; reading is a key to knowledge.

10. **Set goals.** Know what you want out of life. How can you expect to reach a destination if you don't know where you're going. In order to hit your target, you must take aim.

IMPORTANT
Use these ideas as tools to help you gain self-confidence. Try different approaches at different times. Reread this page often as a confidence booster.

Now, let's determine what you need to do to study for the GED.

STEP 3 | DETERMINE WHAT YOU NEED TO STUDY

ATTITUDE IS IMPORTANT

The key to determining if you will get the GED has nothing to do with the actual tests, but everything to do with yourself. Many people fail to get the GED because they give up on themselves. That's why Step 2 offered you ideas and suggestions to boost your self-confidence. Step 3 builds on that self-confidence by helping you develop the right **attitude.**

As you prepare, keep in mind that your goal is not just passing a test. You're really preparing to learn, to grow, and to develop as a person. Do as much as you can to make your GED goal a stepping stone to other positive things in your life—such as obtaining a new job or going on to college.

Before you start studying, you must know where you're starting from. All of your previous education, training, and learning will be helpful to you on the GED. Get to know your strengths and weaknesses, so that you can work to improve the areas that need it.

You'll be taking some sample tests in this section. Your results will help you determine what you need to study for the GED.

> "If you believe you can or if you believe you can't, either way you're right."
> —*Henry Ford*

THREE KEYS TO THE GED

You will recall that the GED tests for three **basic** skills: reading, language, and mathematics.

The Social Studies Test, the Science Test, and the Literature and the Arts Test all involve reading. The test-taker reads passages and answers questions about the passages. The Writing Skills Test evaluates language skills, and the Mathematics Tests, of course, measures mathematics skills.

The following sample tests cover these three areas. They will help you assess your strengths and weaknesses in the three key areas.

LANGUAGE SAMPLE TEST I: PART A

Spelling/Capitalization

Find the misspelled word:

a	b	c	d	e
0	0	0	0	0

1. a. happiness
   b. occassion
   c. joyous
   d. laughter
   e. no error

a	b	c	d	e
0	0	0	0	0

2. a. curiculum
   b. understanding
   c. yesterday
   d. curiosity
   e. no error

a	b	c	d	e
0	0	0	0	0

3. a. agony
   b. empathy
   c. canoeing
   d. hindrence
   e. no error

a	b	c	d	e
0	0	0	0	0

4. a. accompany
   b. independence
   c. vitality
   d. trueth
   e. no error

a	b	c	d	e
0	0	0	0	0

5. a. Wednesday
   b. hopefully
   c. Minneapolis
   d. judgment
   e. no error

Grammar

Find the error:

a	b	c	d	e
0	0	0	0	0

6. Tim and <u>he</u> <u>like</u> the movie very much, but <u>they</u>
          a   b   c

   thought it was <u>too</u> short. <u>no error</u>
                  d   e

a	b	c	d	e
0	0	0	0	0

7. Jim wants Sue and I to help him paint his
         a   b   c   d

   new house. no error
             e

a	b	c	d	e
0	0	0	0	0

8. Whatever John does he does good, though his
              a   b

   methods are somewhat different. no error
     c   d   e

a	b	c	d	e
0	0	0	0	0

9. If their not leaving with Tom and her, maybe
       a   b

   they would like to go with us. no error
     c   d   e

a	b	c	d	e
0	0	0	0	0

10. I don't know how badly she did on the test,
             a   b

    but I'm sure I did worse. no error
          c   d   e

a	b	c	d	e
0	0	0	0	0

11. Every Summer, we vacation in Washington D.C.,
        a   b   c

    which is the capitol of the United States.
             d   e

Sentence Structure

Pick the correct answer:

a	b	c	d	e
0	0	0	0	0

12. I used to trust Doug however, now I know better.

    a. Doug however, now
    b. Doug however; now
    c. Doug; however, now
    d. Doug however now
    e. Doug, however, now

LANGUAGE SAMPLE TEST I (Continued)

a b c d e
0 0 0 0 0

13. Pete doesn't like <u>me I</u> wonder why.

    a. me I
    b. me, I
    c. me yet I
    d. me; and I
    e. me. I

a b c d e
0 0 0 0 0

14. Not only Scott but also Leroy <u>is bringing his</u> wife to the meeting.

    a. is bringing his
    b. is taking his
    c. is taking their
    d. will bring their
    e. are bringing their

a b c d e
0 0 0 0 0

15. A person should keep very busy when <u>you are</u> depressed.

    a. you are
    b. she is
    c. they are
    d. their
    e. it is

GED Language Review: Answers and Results

Answers

1. b	
2. a	
3. d	
4. d	
5. e	
6. b	
7. b	
8. b	
9. a	
10. e	
11. a	
12. c	
13. e	
14. b	
15. b	

Results

Your number right

15-13   Great! You have a good chance of passing the Writing Skills Test with a high score.

12-8   Very Good! You probably need some review. But you should be able to pass the test.

7 and below   Good! Yet, you'll most likely need to review the areas of sentence structure, grammar, and punctuation.

Note: Generally, if you can answer half of the questions right on a GED test, you'll receive a passing score of 45.

LANGUAGE SAMPLE TEST I: PART B

On the next page, write a full-page letter to someone you know. Follow these guidelines as you write the letter:

- Write at least three paragraphs.

- In the first paragraph, describe how nice it was to hear from your friend. Then tell him or her about what you've been doing.

- In the second paragraph, tell your friend about your desire to get the GED, what you're doing to achieve it, and what you'll do after you get it.

- In the third paragraph, ask your friend to visit soon and describe some areas in your city or town you'd like to show him or her.

- Make sure each sentence begins with a capital letter and has end pucnctuation.

- Make sure that what you write makes sense!

On the actual GED tests, the content of what you write and the way you write it is important. Ask a friend or parent to read your letter to see that it meets the guidelines above.

If your letter satisfies the guidelines, you'll do well on the Writing Skills Essay Test. If it doesn't, it's a good idea for you to review language skills and practice writing.

A LETTER TO A FRIEND

Make sure each sentence is complete, makes sense, and relates to or fits with the other sentences.

Date: _____

Dear _____ ,

Sincerely,

_____

READING SAMPLE, TEST I

GED READING PASSAGE

Getting a job can be hard, but it is also rewarding. By using good job-seeking skills, you will be successful. Finding a job in today's marketplace is especially difficult for people changing careers and for young people. But jobs are available. And there are ways for you to get the job you desire.

It's important to know what you want, to have good job-seeking skills, and to keep a positive attitude. Follow these tips as you look to find the job that's best for you:

1. **Be positive about your talents and skills.** Your greatest asset is your attitude. Don't disqualify yourself for a job you want. Give yourself credit for all your skills. Many people never try for certain jobs because they decide that they aren't qualified even before checking out the job.

2. **Know yourself.** Review your skills, experiences, hobbies, education, and interests. Make a list of your strengths and positive qualities. Identify the areas where you need to improve. This will help you decide which jobs you can do.

3. **Learn about the jobs you want to have.** Read about them or ask others for information. What qualifications are required? How do these positions fit with what you can do now? What additional training or experience do you need? Where can you get the job? Where do you begin?

4. **Use the "Help Wanted" ads only as a first step.** Contact all the companies with jobs that fit your list. Want ads only give you a snapshot of what's available. Many good jobs are never advertised. Tell all of your friends, neighbors, and relatives that you are job hunting. This is called networking. Most job seekers find jobs through the network of contacts they develop.

5. **Add your name to job prospect lists.** Contact high school or college counselors, private employment services, and government programs. Also, there are job placement services run by city, county, state, and federal offices. This is also part of networking and a way to get exposure to many job opportunities.

6. **Contact all possible employers properly.** Most employers require a phone call, application, resume, or all three. Use the best approach for each particular job. Many times you can call the company and ask for the manager in charge of the job you want. Ask for the manager's name and its correct spelling and the complete address of the company.

7. **Organize all the information you need for the job search.** Have an updated resume, letters of recommendation, or at least three references with addresses and phone numbers, drivers license number, social security number, addresses of past jobs, employment dates, and school addresses. Use this information for the application and interview.

8. **Ask for interviews.** This is the most important step in the job search. Interviews lead to job offers. If you send a letter, ask for an interview. If you talk to the manager on the phone, ask for an interview.

9. **Learn about the company where you will interview.** Read company brochures. Think about the kinds of questions the interviewer might ask. Plan how you will answer. Practice this ahead of time. And prepare to ask a few good questions so that you will understand the job and what is expected of the person who takes it.

10. **Be courteous and confident during the interview.** Sell yourself in an honest way. Talk about your strengths. Some nervousness is natural. Control it by relaxing and making eye contact with the interviewer. Answer all questions as specifically as possible. Remember to have a neat appearance and to smile!

READING SAMPLE TEST I (Continued)

11. **Practice how to interview.** Ask friends or relatives to rehearse "pretend" interviews with you. Practicing your interview technique makes you better prepared during actual interviews. In a "live" interview, let the interviewer control the meeting, but answer all questions fully—don't just answer questions with a "yes" or "no." Emphasize your good points. Be prepared for questions concerning why you left a company, why you haven't worked in a while, or about one of your weaknesses.

12. **Follow up after every interview.** After every interview, send a neatly written thank you note. Then, call the interviewer back within a week.

13. **Be persistent.** If you don't get a job after an interview, don't be discouraged. Review what you did right. Pick one thing to do better next time. Keep looking for a job and asking for interviews. Keep believing in yourself. And follow these 13 tips with a positive attitude, and eventually you'll get the job you desire and deserve.

GED READING PASSAGE: QUESTIONS

Answer the following questions based on the passage above. You can look back in the passage for the answers. Shade in the best answer.

a b c d e
0 0 0 0 0

1. Which of the following is the best title for the passage?

    a. "Start with the Help Wanted Ads—And Go From There"
    b. "A Tight Job Market Makes Job Hunting Difficult"
    c. "The Interview—The Most Important Step in Job Hunting"
    d. "Thirteen Tips on Finding the Best Job for You"
    e. "Keep the Job you Have"

a b c d e
0 0 0 0 0

2. According to the passage, "Help Wanted" ads:

    a. list all jobs.
    b. are the only place to look for work.
    c. are only a starting place to look for work.
    d. are not a very good place to look for work.
    e. help most people get new jobs.

a b c d e
0 0 0 0 0

3. It's most important for you to know your strengths and weaknesses because:

    a. it will help you decide on the jobs you can do.
    b. it will help you better understand employers.
    c. it will help you decide on many jobs you could never do.
    d. it will help an employer decide if you're right for a job.
    e. you'll know what not to tell an employer.

```
a  b  c  d  e
0  0  0  0  0
```
4. The passage says that you should keep a positive attitude. This means you should:

   a. exaggerate to others what you can really do.
   b. believe in yourself and talk about what you can do.
   c. pretend that you have skills you don't have.
   d. never recognize or admit a mistake.
   e. forget past mistakes.

```
a  b  c  d  e
0  0  0  0  0
```
5. A placement office is:

   a. a place to get your social security card.
   b. a public or private agency that will help you find a job.
   c. a place to collect unemployment checks.
   d. a place where the government will give you a job.
   e. none of the above.

```
a  b  c  d  e
0  0  0  0  0
```
6. The most important step in looking for a job is:

   a. filling out the application.
   b. the use of the Help Wanted ads.
   c. the interview.
   d. a letter of reference.
   e. none of the above.

```
a  b  c  d  e
0  0  0  0  0
```
7. You might need all of the following during your job search except a:

   a. drivers license.
   b. reference list.
   c. resume.
   d. marriage certificate.
   e. permit.

READING SAMPLE TEST I (Continued)

a b c d e
0 0 0 0 0

8. A job hunter should do all of the following except:

    a. use the Help Wanted ads as the only source for job leads.
    b. ask some questions during the interview.
    c. tell everyone she knows that she is looking for work.
    d. research the company he is interested in.
    e. put his name on waiting lists.

a b c d e
0 0 0 0 0

9. Which of the following things should you do in an interview:

    a. smoke when you want to.
    b. answer all questions with a yes or no.
    c. have good eye contact.
    d. do all the talking.
    e. don't ask any questions.

a b c d e
0 0 0 0 0

10. During the course of an interview you should:

    a. sell yourself.
    b. do anything you can to get the job.
    c. tell the employer only about what he asks for.
    d. tell the employer you can do any job in the company.
    e. all of the above

GED Reading: Answers and Results

Answers

1. d
2. c
3. a
4. b
5. b
6. c
7. d
8. a
9. c
10. a

Results

Your number right

10-9   Great! You have a good chance of passing the GED reading tests without any trouble.

8-6   Very Good! You probably need some review. But you should be able to pass the reading tests or at least come close.

5 & less   Average. However, you'll most likely need to review and improve your reading skills before you can pass the tests. How much you'll need to review will depend on your attitude and the specific skills you need to improve.

MATH SAMPLE TEST I

GED MATH REVIEW

Whole numbers

1
$$16 \atop +32$$

$$242 \atop +79$$

2
$$45 \atop -12$$

$$121 \atop -59$$

3
$$6 \atop \times 9$$

$$7 \atop \times 7$$

$$22 \atop \times 8$$

$$231 \atop \times 24$$

4 $5\overline{)\,.30}$ $9\overline{)\,4527}$ $23\overline{)\,163}$ $28\overline{)\,7028}$

5 $(5 \times 9) + (8 \div 2) - (4) =$

Fractions

6
$$1\,1/4 \atop +1\,1/4$$

7
$$2\,1/4 \atop +\ 3/8$$

8
$$2 \atop -\,5/6$$

9
$$3\,3/4 \atop +1\,3/4$$

10 $1/4 \times 1/2 =$

11 $2\,2/3 \times 1\,1/3 =$ **12** $2 \times 1/3 =$ **13** $1/4 \div 5 =$

14 $1/4 \div 3/8 =$ **15**   Which fraction is smallest: 1/2, 6/11, 11/21 or 9/19?

Decimals

16   (.241) Write this as a word: **17**   Write in decimal form fifteen hundredths =

18   Which decimal is larger?   .005, .050, .125, .35   **19**
$$\$5.35 \atop +2.31$$

20   You have $20.00 to spend on groceries, and you received $2.18 in change. How much were the groceries?

MATH SAMPLE TEST I (Continued)

Percent

21 5.2
       ×31

22 .35$\overline{)1.575}$

23 .35 = _____%

24 .33 1/3 = _____%

25 50% = _____ decimal form

26 66 2/3% = _____fraction form

27 5/8 = _____ decimal

PLEASE CIRCLE YOUR ANSWERS

5/8 = _____ percent

GED MATH REVIEW: ANSWERS

Whole numbers

1 16   242   **2** 45   121   **3** 6   7   22   231
    +32   +79   −12   −59   ×9   ×7   ×8   ×24
   ───   ───   ───   ───   ──   ──   ───   ───
    48   321   33   62   54   49   176   924
                                                                             4620
                                                                             ────
                                                                             5544

4 $\overset{.06}{5\overline{)\,.30}}$ $\overset{503}{9\overline{)\,4527}}$ $\overset{7\ r2}{23\overline{)\,163}}$ $\overset{251}{28\overline{)\,7028}}$
                                                          161   56xx
                                                          ───   ───
                                                            2   142
                                                                               140
                                                                               ───
                                                                                28

5 (5×9) + (8÷2) − (4) =
        45 +   4   − 4 = 45

Fractions

6 1 1/4   **7** 2 1/4 = 2/8   **8** 2 = 1 6/6   **9** 3 3/4   **10** 1/4 × 1/2 = 1/8
    +1 1/4   + 3/8   −5/6   +1 3/4
   ──────   ──────   ────   ──────
   2 2/4 =2 1/2   2 5/8   1 1/6   4 6/4 = 5 2/4 = 5 1/2

11 2 2/3 × 1 1/3 =   **12** 2 × 1/3 = 2/3   **13** 1/4 ÷ 5 = 1/4 × 1/5 = 1/20
     8/3 × 4/3 = 32/9 = 3 5/9

14 1/4 ÷ 3/8 =   **15** 1/2
     1/4 × 8/3 = 8/12 = 2/3

Decimals

16 (.241) Write this as a word:
two hundred forty-one thousandths

17 Write in decimal form fifteen hundredths = .15

18 Which decimal is larger?   .35

19 $5.35
    +2.31
    $7.66

20 You have $20.00 to spend on groceries, and you received $2.18 in change. How much were the groceries? $17.82

Percent

21   5.2
       ×.31
       52
       1560
       1.612

22   4.5
    .35) 1.575
         140
         175
         175

23   .35 = 35%

24 .33 1/3 = 33 1/3%

25 50% = .50   decimal form

26 66 2/3% = 2/3 fraction form

27 5/8 = .625 decimal

5/8 = 62.5 %

GED Math Test: Answers and Results

Your number right

36-30   Great! You should pass the GED math test without any trouble.

30-20   Very good! You can do enough math so that you'll need limited review before you pass the test.

19 and below   Average. But you'll need to review fractions, decimals and percent before you'll pass the test.

Note: Generally, if you can answer half the questions right on a GED test, you'll get a passing score of 45. On the Math Test you must know how to do whole numbers, fractions, decimals and percents in word problem situations (as in question 20). And, remember, math problems will be multiple choice questions.

WHAT YOU NEED TO STUDY: KEY AREAS

LANGUAGE SKILLS	READING SKILLS	MATH SKILLS
Spelling	Identifying the main idea	Whole numbers
Subject and predicate	Identifying supporting	• add/subtract
Verb usage	details	• multiply/divide
Nouns/pronouns	Drawing conclusions	Fractions
Punctuation	Applying ideas	Decimals
Capitalization	Style and tone	Percents
Logic and organization	Following directions	Reading graphs
	Comprehension	Algebraic equations
		Geometry

SUGGESTIONS TO IMPROVE YOUR GED SCORECARD

1. If you had about half right or less on any one of the sample tests, you'll need to review the seven skills indicated in the test area above. Purchase a GED review book at a bookstore or use one from the library, and do practice exercises in the area where you're weak.

2. If you had 2/3 or more of the questions right, you'll probably pass the GED tests without any trouble. (If you had only 1 or 2 wrong in *all* the areas, take the GED tests soon after you follow Step 3.) Usually one area gives people trouble. For example, if math is hard for you, do practice exercises in math. Again, purchase a GED review book, use one from the library, or get help from an adult education program.

3. Take time to read before you take the GED tests, regardless of the results of the tests you took in this book. Reading is the most important area because all the tests require you to read and follow instructions to complete them. The average reading level on the GED tests is similar to what's necessary to read most newspapers.

From now on read as much as you can. Read the newspaper. Read your favorite magazine or book. Take a few minutes after you read to recall the important points. Try to remember the key ideas. The GED tests require you to do this. Although you can always look back in a reading selection to find the main ideas, you'll need to be able to sit and read for up to 1½ hours at a time.

YOUR SCORE CARD

COMMENTS

		(Write in here what you did well and areas you need to improve.)
	MATH	
	I II	
Total Possible	1. 36	
Your score	2.	
	READING	
	I II	
Total Possible	1. 10	
Your score	2.	
	LANGUAGE	
	I II	
Total Possible	1. 15	
Your score	2.	
	KEY AREAS	
What you need to study		

Congratulations! You have completed three steps to the GED Formula for Success.

Step 4 will help you form a plan to achieve your goal. You'll receive specific advice on how to study and how to take the GED tests. Don't stop now; you're almost there!

Note: A second step of sample tests for each area is found at the end of the book. After some study and review, take them to check your progress.

SUCCESS STORY #3:
MARY'S HOPE

Many years ago, Mary dropped out of school in her senior year because she was getting married. She stayed home and over the years raised seven children. When the youngest was in kindergarten. Mary, in her 40s, got a job in a cleaning service at a hotel.

She began to think that maybe after all these years, she'd like to finish the education that had been interrupted years before. But could she do it? It had been such a long time since school that the prospect of taking tests again scared her. After talking to a teacher in adult education, Mary was confident she could do it. Reading, she learned, was a key to doing well in the tests. Since she had always been an avid reader, it helped her gain the confidence to take the test.

She purchased a GED review book from a local bookstore and took a stab at it, soon realizing that with her years of experience, she had to study only a short time. When she took the tests, she passed easily.

Now in her mid-50s, Mary trains frontline employees at a restaurant. She's also preparing to enter college to continue her education.

STEP 4 | MAKE A PLAN TO ACHIEVE YOUR GOAL

ESTABLISHING A GOAL

Now's the time to get specific about your GED plan. So far you have:

- Identified the benefits of the GED to you
- Worked on gaining the confidence to work at getting the GED and achieving your other desires
- Determined your reading, language, and math strengths and weaknesses on the GED sample tests so you know what you need to study.

Following are some questions you must answer to help you complete this final step:

- What are my study habits?
- Do I know how to take tests?
- If I need additional help, where can I go?
- What's a goal I have beyond the GED?
- When will I take the tests?
- Where will I take the tests?
- Am I committed to passing the tests and earning a high school equivalency certificate?

YOUR GED GOAL CONTRACT

Complete this goal contract to help you achieve the GED. Sign and date it.

1. Target Date to get the GED: _____

   (See pages 1-39 to see how you already responded to the following.)

2. Why I want the GED: _____

3. Benefits I receive with the GED: _____

4. These positive traits will help me get my GED:

   - _____
   - _____
   - _____

YOUR GED GOAL CONTRACT
(Continued)

5. Study Areas

Language		Reading		Math	
Strengths	Improvement Needed	Strengths	Improvement Needed	Strengths	Improvement Needed

(You'll find information on the items below on pages 43-56.)

6. Study Habits

Helpful study habits _____

Habits to avoid _____

7. Method of Study

When _____

How _____

Do I need more help? Where? _____

8. Test-Taking Tips (check if read 3 times) _____

9. One thing I really love _____

10. A goal beyond the GED is _____

11. Where I'll take the GED tests

Place _____ Address _____

Phone number _____ Cost _____

My appointment date _____

12. Your Name _____ Date _____

GED SUCCESS CHART

Am I willing to:	high willingness			low willingness	
1. Get help from others?	5	4	3	2	1
2. Study regularly?	5	4	3	2	1
3. Learn new things?	5	4	3	2	1
4. Make mistakes?	5	4	3	2	1
5. Practice new skills?	5	4	3	2	1
6. Read, read, read?	5	4	3	2	1
7. Listen to others?	5	4	3	2	1
8. Ask questions of others?	5	4	3	2	1
9. Take tests?	5	4	3	2	1
10. Learn from others?	5	4	3	2	1
11. Get things done on my own?	5	4	3	2	1
12. Take risks?	5	4	3	2	1

COMMENT

All these areas are important in reviewing for the GED. The more willing you are to do them, the easier it will be for you to get the GED and to learn and progress in other matters as well.

SELF-EVALUATION: STUDY HABITS

Circle each "yes" that applies to you. Be honest. This inventory quickly identifies your strengths and weaknesses for study and test taking. Do this to help keep your confidence up and to identify additional obstacles.

1. I enjoy reading.   YES
2. I am easily distracted.   YES
3. I make friends easily.   YES
4. I get tired easily.   YES
5. I like a challenge.   YES
6. I am on a tight schedule.   YES
7. I am a good planner.   YES
8. I am easily embarassed.   YES
9. I like learning.   YES
10. I watch TV often.   YES
11. I have some free time.   YES
12. I talk on the phone often.   YES
13. I am able to work alone.   YES
14. I am afraid to make mistakes.   YES
15. I am able to finish what I start.   YES
16. I have difficulty sleeping.   YES

SUMMARY

The more *ODD* items you circled YES, the greater your chance of working hard to complete the GED. The more *EVEN* items you circled YES, the harder you'll have to work to get the GED.

THREE WAYS TO STUDY

Three ways to prepare for the GED are:
- Prepare alone
- Study with another person
- Attend a GED prep program

1. PREPARE ALONE

By reading this book, you have already chosen this route. People who follow this method can usually pass the tests if they stay motivated. That's how the four steps in the Formula for Success are geared to help you.

If you need review in skills areas after you finish this book, check out a GED book from the library (or buy one at a local bookstore). Then, study the skill areas in the sample tests in which you scored low. Schedule regular times to review. Study at times you won't be distracted. Get help from relatives or friends if you need it. Review an area until you can get one-half or more of the questions right. Then follow your GED goal plan and go take the tests. Don't forget to be confident. You can do it!

2. STUDY WITH ANOTHER PERSON

By studying with another person, you can support each other by helping each other in the difficult areas. If you are good in math and your partner is poor in math, then you can help him or her. Likewise, if you are poor in answering reading questions and your partner is good at it, then he or she can help you. Having a partner can help you stick with it when you want to quit.

3. ATTEND A GED PREP PROGRAM

If you need a lot of practice in a skill area, a GED Prep Program may be helpful, and it's not the same as returning to school. Most GED programs are set up differently from schools: no bells, grades, or detentions. The instructors are trained to help you. Most classes are held one to two nights a week. Some schools have day classes. Classes usually last one to two hours and are informal. You can attend when you want to. You don't have to recite in class or work on a chalkboard. You'll be on a first-name basis with the instructor. The instructor will take the time to get to know what will work best for you.

In most cases, the instructor will give you a test to find out in what areas you do well and what you need to work on. Only you and the instructor will know your test results. Then the instructor will help you study and learn. The instructor is a resource for you. Ask questions; your instructor will answer them.

If you need to study for the GED, you'll find that some areas will be easier than others. Be patient. Expect to learn. Give yourself time to make learning a habit again. Think of things you do everyday that you can relate to the GED. Make the review apply to as many of these situations as possible.

TEST-TAKING TIPS

Before you take the GED test, read the test tips below at least *three* times. Experience shows that you can add up to five points on your test score if you follow these tips.

The GED is called a power test. This means that it is a test that is designed to test competency in basic skills. It is also a timed test.

You should study these points, since they will help you get a better score on the GED:

A. How to get yourself calmed down on the day of the test.
B. How to read the GED test.
C. How to answer the GED test.
D. How to go back over the test.

A. Try to be calm on the day of the test. In other words, try to do what you can to do your best. Listed below are some helpful hints:
  1. Get a good night's rest before the test.
  2. Dress in clothes that are comfortable.
  3. Eat a good meal before testing, but one that is fairly light.
  4. Get to the testing center early so you can get used to the surroundings.
  5. Listen to the test administrator and write down any key points.
  6. Expect to be somewhat nervous on the day of the test but know what it takes for you to relax.

B. Listed below are some suggestions that will help you perform better on the GED test.
  7. The test is scored by number correct only. There is no penalty for incorrect answers, so guess if you have to. Don't leave any questions blank.
  8. Read all instructions carefully.
  9. Follow the instructions carefully.
  10. Watch out for useless and distracting information on the test.
  11. Watch for "twists" such as "all the following are true except..."
  12. Read all answers quickly and select one. Waiting too long to answer can waste time.
  13. Watch for subject/verb agreement in the grammar section (He *is*...not, he *are*...).
  14. Look for clues to help you with an answer such as:
    a) All/Always/never/none—the answer must fit every case.
    b) The use of a/an may tip you. A word that begins with a consonant follows the word "a" and a word that begins with a vowel follows the word "an."

15. Read questions carefully to understand exactly what is called for or seems right.
16. Don't use your opinion to answer questions. Use the writer's opinion; answers are based on passages *as written.*
17. Don't expect all answers to follow a logical sequence in the word problems or reading passages.
18. Don't worry if a subject deals with topics with which you're not familiar. Just read the passage and answer the questions the best you can.

C. Listed below are some tips to help you *answer* the test better:
19. First, answer all the questions you know for sure.
20. Eliminate answers that are clearly wrong.
21. Where two or more answers seem possible, select what you think is the best one and compare it to the others as a way to check.
22. On the true or false multiple choice questions, follow these suggestions:
    a) A statement is false *if any part of it* is false.
    b) Watch out for words like ''sometimes'' and ''occasionally.''
23. Answer every question on the test, even if you must guess.
24. Keep an eye on time! Do the questions you know first; then go back and guess on the others. Don't get bogged down (one minute is tops). Go on to the next question. Use a ''?'' next to the questions needing further review.
25. Follow these 6 steps in answering problem questions and reading passages:
    a) Scan passage quickly to get the main idea.
    b) Reread the problem carefully and see what facts are given. Underline key points.
    c) Read the question; look for the answer in the text. Determine which facts apply.
    d) Decide how to use the main idea or key points to answer the question.
    e) Carefully apply the information and pick an answer to the question.
    f) Check your work, but remember to budget your time and don't take too much time on any one problem.

D. Follow the steps below to check the test when you finish:
26. Leave at least 1/10 of the time for checking.
27. An important key is to check the instructions on a question.
28. Check your answer sheet for the correct placement of your answers.
29. Look with special care at the tougher questions.
30. Answer all questions that you left blank and marked with a ''?.''
31. Guess by eliminating the possible answers that are obviously wrong.
32. Only change your answer if you are positive that you are right the second time.
33. Finally, keep a positive attitude throughout the test.

SUCCESS STORY #4:
HAROLD'S GOAL

Harold quit school years ago to join the army. Marriage followed, and after his tour of service, he began to work as a machinist. Twenty years and six children later, Harold began to think about the future. By this time, he was also a recovering alcoholic and felt the need to contribute to society and to work with his mind rather than his hands only.

Harold needed to start back at the beginning and pick up the high school diploma he'd never gotten. He took a correspondence course to prepare him for the GED, passed the tests, and became a counselor.

His success in this new career gave him more confidence and spurred him to enroll in college, where he received a degree. Today, he's not only an expert in the field of chemical dependence but heads the entire program at a well-known chemical dependence treatment facility.

ADDITIONAL HELPFUL RESOURCES

If you need additional help with your GED review, that's OK. Seeking help is important if you want it. Successful people get others to help them build on their strengths and to help them improve where needed. Take a risk and get the help you need. It'll help you get the GED and achieve your other goals sooner. Remember, getting the GED is a key to your future!

There are a number of places to go for help. You'll want to seek help fairly close to home, with hours that fit your needs. Call around. Ask the different schools or agencies what they can do for you.

Most GED programs and their teachers are truly interested in helping you, but sometimes they don't know how. That's why it's important for you to know yourself. Do everything you can do to study on your own. Then, attend GED programs for specific help. For example, if you need to learn to divide fractions or work on spelling, ask for help in these problem areas.

An advantage of attending a GED program is that materials will be available and copies of the practice material can be taken home.

In a good GED program, teachers will be interested in you as a person. The classroom will be informal, without a ''schoolroom'' atmosphere. You won't be asked to take long tests. And you won't be told to review books from the beginning to the end. You'll be asked to review areas that you forgot or need to brush up on. The teachers will give you individual attention and have some group activity. A good GED program will be a place where you can relax, get comfortable, and learn quickly.

Sometimes, group activity helps you learn quickly. In group activity, people support one another in learning. It's helpful to get as much support as you can while you review for the GED. In many group activities you'll find that other people have the same questions and needs that you have. Give it a try. Participate. Do something new. Ask some questions. Get help. Give help. You'll find the support you need to get the GED. And you'll be able to support others in their efforts. In the next few pages are descriptions of places that might be of help to you.

ADDITIONAL HELPFUL RESOURCES
(Continued)

LOCAL HIGH SCHOOL

Call your local high school. Ask for the director of adult or community education. She or he will be glad to help you find a GED program and can direct you to the nearest GED testing center.

LOCAL COLLEGE

Contact your local college. Many times, colleges serve as GED testing centers. Talk to a guidance counselor or the director of the college's evening program. They will be able to help you with questions about the GED and can give you ideas about furthering your training or education, too.

VOCATIONAL TECHNICAL SCHOOL

Check with a vocational technical school near you. A counselor usually has information about GED classes that are held in the community or similar review classes may be held at the vocational school itself.

LOCAL BOOK STORE

Many book stores sell books for in-depth GED preparation and study. Most of the books sell for under $15.00. Publishers include Barron's, Arco, Contemporary Books, and Scott Foresman.

TELEVISION

In many cities today, cable TV or public TV broadcast GED preparation programs. Check your local TV guides for the dates and times of programs in your area.

STATE DEPARTMENT OF EDUCATION

Call or write your state's Department of Education. Look in the white pages of the phone book for their number. Usually there will be a special section in the phone book for government offices, often in the front of the book.

The best place to get information on the GED will be in the adult education section of your state's Department of Education. People who work in this department should know of GED classes and testing centers in your state.

FEDERAL GOVERNMENT

The Department of Education in Washington, D.C., also has information on the GED. Write or call the Adult Education Division: Department of Education, Humphrey Building, 400 Independence Ave., SW, Washington, D.C., 20202; (202) 245-3192.

THE AMERICAN COUNCIL ON EDUCATION

This federal agency runs the nationwide GED testing program. It also develops the GED tests. Call or write them and ask for information on the GED: The American Council on Education, The GED Testing Service, One Dupont Circle, Washington, D.C., 20036; (202) 939-9490.

FEDERAL INFORMATION CENTERS

A number of federal information centers exist throughout the country. Look in the phone book for the telephone number of the one nearest you. Ask about GED preparation and testing in your state.

ARMED SERVICES

Consider joining the Navy, Army, Airforce or Marines. Often, they will help you get the GED. Be aware that the armed services only allow a limited number of people to join without a high school diploma. So check it out first. You might need to get the GED before you join.

LIBRARIES

Some libraries have in-depth GED review books that you can borrow for free. Good videotapes are also sometimes available from public libraries.

EXTRA PROGRAMS

Many times businesses, city programs, or federally funded agencies will offer additional help. Many government job programs have GED classes available; the Job Corps and 70001 offer GED classes. Some businesses offer GED classes to help their employees improve their basic skills. Cities sometimes sponsor GED programs, especially for the unemployed. See if your city is offering a program that might help you.

A SUMMARY

All of the resources described above, and others, can provide help to you in your effort to get your GED. Some of them provide literature; others sponsor classes that prepare you to take the GED examination. They may not always provide help as quickly as you would like, but be patient—and persistent! Their help is usually free—but it will be worth a lot to you.

WORDS OF WISDOM:
WHAT TO DO ONCE THE GED IS YOURS

Congratulations! You've worked hard to complete this book. Now take the GED tests or finish your final review. Go for it and get the most from your efforts. When you're ready to take the test, for the best results, do so within two to three weeks after finishing this book.

It's helpful to know what you want to do once the test is behind you. In fact, knowing where you want to go can really help get you there: Motivation is a key part of every success story. This step may help you even if you already know where you want to go.

AREA #1: THINGS YOU LOVE

Successful people are successful, according to several studies, because they know what they love. They know the things that turn them on in life. Someone once said, ''People don't stop working and playing because they are old; they get old because they stop working and playing.''

Too many people are stuck in jobs or situations they don't like. Naturally, they aren't very happy. Sometimes they try to ''lose themselves'' in their work or in watching too much TV. Why not get involved in activities that you really enjoy? Check off ☑ the following activities that you like doing—and then, **DO THEM!**

☐ reading   ☐ visiting museums
☐ camping   ☐ writing letters
☐ biking   ☐ taking trips
☐ walking   ☐ making crafts
☐ eating out   ☐ hiking
☐ drawing   ☐ learning something new
☐ woodworking   ☐ spending time with a special person
☐ working out   ☐ playing with children
☐ visiting friends ☐ swimming
☐ helping the needy ☐ cooking
☐ gardening   ☐ other _____
☐ dancing

Fill out the chart below and plan to do the things you love. You'll be happier and more satisfied in life.

I love...	Last time I did this	Next time I'll do it
1.		
2.		
3.		
4.		
5.		
6.		
7.		
8.		

AREA #2: SETTING GOALS

Successful people set goals and write their goals on paper. A goal is something a person wants to do, have, or be. Usually, a goal requires that a person learn, grow, develop, and work hard. Look at goals this way:

G—Great
O—Opportunties
A—to Achieve
L—to Learn and
S—to Succeed

Goals fire your desire to get more out of life. Goals make you take action. They inspire you to go from where you are to where you want to be.

Motivator Zig Ziglar says, ''Goal setting is a process that enables you to consciously and intentionally shape your future.''

What are your goals? What do you want your future to be? A critical step to a successful future beyond the GED is to plan for it. You have the opportunity in this book. Don't leave your future to chance. As Louis Pasteur said, ''Chance favors the prepared mind.''

On the next page, list your goals in the six major goal areas. Goals others have set as they prepared to get their GEDs include:

FAMILY/SOCIAL   To get married within three years.

CAREER   To get a new job as an assistant manager within six months.

SPIRITUAL   To read the Bible daily.

FINANCIAL   To save $1,000 in a year.

MENTAL   To start vocational school in the fall.

PHYSICAL   To lose 20 pounds in the next few months.

A goal has to be specific (to get a new job as an assistant manager). It must be realistic. Becoming a millionaire overnight, while a delightful thought, isn't realistic—unless you win a lottery! Finally, it needs a time frame (within six months).

GOALS

Family/Social
(relating to family or friends)

short range (6 mo.)

long range (3 yrs.)

Financial
(money matters)

short range (6 mo.)

long range (3 yrs.)

Career
(affecting my job)

short range (6 mo.)

long range (3 yrs.)

Mental
(further education or learning)

short range (6 mo.)

long range (3 yrs.)

Spiritual
(affecting my beliefs)

short range (6 mo.)

long range (3 yrs.)

Physical
(health and recreation)

short range (6 mo.)

long range (3 yrs.)

AREA #3: TAKING CONTROL

Many people feel that they don't have what they want in life for reasons apart from themselves. They tend to say things like this:

- "My parents didn't understand me."
- "Nobody helps me."
- "There is no opportunity."
- "Teachers were out to get me."
- "My boss doesn't care."
- "I'm a loser."

The truth is that you get out of life what you put into. Your life is your responsibility. Get training or an education if you need it. Ask for help if you want it. Try new things to get better results. Take action; take control.

Thousands of people have pulled themselves up from poverty and a lack of education and other obstacles to succeed. You can, too. Don't let anything defeat you. Have a burning desire to be all that you can be.

Thomas Wolfe wrote: "If a man has a talent and cannot use it, he has failed. If he has a talent and uses only half of it, he has partly failed. If he has a talent and learns somehow to use the whole of it, he has gloriously succeeded and won a satisfaction and triumph few men ever know."

It's too easy to blame other people or other situations. Start with yourself. Believe that as you learn new things and try new things, you'll get more out of life. Do what you love, reach for your goals, take control, and you'll go far beyond the GED. Good luck.

APPENDIX

THE LANGUAGE SAMPLE TEST II

Capitalization

Choose the words that should always be capitalized:

a	b	c	d	e
0	0	0	0	0

1. a. cemetery
   b. hospital
   c. school
   d. denver
   e. judge

a	b	c	d	e
0	0	0	0	0

2. a. priest
   b. teacher
   c. monday
   d. lawyer
   e. constitution

a	b	c	d	e
0	0	0	0	0

3. a. student
   b. dan
   c. boy
   d. father
   e. none of the above

Grammar and Punctuation

Find the error:

a	b	c	d	e
0	0	0	0	0

4. Pete and Sue cried all day when there
            a   b   c

   father died. no error
        d   e

a	b	c	d	e
0	0	0	0	0

5. Let's go to the movies. Brendan wants
       a   b

   to go, to. no error
    c   d   e

THE LANGUAGE SAMPLE TEST II (Continued)

a b c d e
0 0 0 0 0

6. The management team has a strong commitment
                      a b

   to succeed and so do the employees. no error
             c   d   e

a b c d e
0 0 0 0 0

7. Even before his feet hit the Las Vegas streets,
                   a   b

   Roland have made his choice to be different.
          c   d

   no error
   e

a b c d e
0 0 0 0 0

8. You might ask yourself_   what kind of careers
                     a

   are not worth pursuing? no error
   b c   d   e

a b c d e
0 0 0 0 0

9. He decided not only to specialize in accounting,
              a

   _but he was quick to try new ideas—for
   b   c

   example_he installed a new computer system
        d

   in the office. no error
                 e

a b c d e
0 0 0 0 0

10. They tried hard to succeed; however she
        a   b   c

    just didn't make it. no error
     d   e

Sentence Structure

a	b	c	d	e
0	0	0	0	0

Pick the correct answer

11. The storms made him <u>despondent; he had</u> developed a sense of calm and the storms reminded him of his difficult past.
    a. despondent, he
    b. despondent, he
    c. despondent—He
    d. despondent: He
    e. no error

a	b	c	d	e
0	0	0	0	0

12. The hockey player swung at the puck a number of <u>time</u> and missed each time.
    a. time's
    b. times
    c. times'
    d. timses
    e. no error

Spelling

a	b	c	d	e
0	0	0	0	0

Find the misspelled word

13. a. beleive
    b. separable
    c. writing
    d. often
    e. Tuesday

a	b	c	d	e
0	0	0	0	0

14. a. busines
    b. beginning
    c. laid
    d. their
    e. enough

a	b	c	d	e
0	0	0	0	0

15. a. lovable
    b. sincerely
    c. approval
    d. advertizement
    e. receive

GED READING SAMPLE TEST II

If someone were to give you $250,000 for your lungs, would you take it? Or, if someone were to give you $500,000 for your heart, would you make a trade? How about $1 million for your brain? So far, no one is seriously interested in such an offer. You can't put a price tag on your lungs, heart or brain, because without them, you die.

However, what is your greatest resource? Is it your lungs? Your heart? Your brain?

One behavioral study stated that 93 percent of the success of an individual is due to his attitude. Only 7 percent of his or her success is due to job knowledge, communications skills, and technical expertise. People with a positive attitude learn what they need to know and get results. Your attitude is your greatest resource.

Here are two positive attitudes worth developing:
• Expect the best of yourself.
• Believe you cannot fail.

EXPECT THE BEST

Can you imagine the results if every time you went fishing you said
• I won't catch anything, as usual.
• I hate sitting in the boat.
• The lakes are too crowded.
• My buddy will screw everything up.
• This is going to be boring.

Would you enjoy fishing? Would you purchase new tackle or try new spots to improve your catch? No way! Your negative attitude has already predicted the results.

In the 1984 Olympics, Mary Lou Retton was down to her last jump in the vault. She was in second place to the East German gymnast. Mary needed a 9.95 to tie for the gold medal. What do you think her attitude was?
• I can't do it?
• My coach is a jerk?
• I'm nervous and scared?

Denis Waitley, motivator and behavioral psychologist, talked to Mary Lou after the event. He learned that she thought about the jump. She had to run hard, extend, tuck and plant. She had done it before and believed she'd do it again. Mary Lou said to herself, "I need a 10. Get a 10. This one is for you, Mom and Dad." She got a 10.

She didn't go for a tie; she went for the gold. She expected the best and achieved the best she could do.

BELIEVE YOU CANNOT FAIL

Your mind will do what you program it to do. Are you setting yourself up for failure or success? A department store was having problems with theft. As a way to combat the problem, the store played a subliminal message with the background music. The message said, ''Don't steal; shoplifters will be prosecuted.'' Shoplifting went up 25 percent. The negative message actually encouraged people to steal. So the store changed the message to say, ''Be nice and honest. Pay at the cashier.'' Shoplifting went down.

What messages do you give yourself or others? Do you always criticize what's happening and complain? It'll set you up for failure: you'll have problems with friends, neighbors and fellow workers. Over time, your thoughts rule your actions. So why not make those thoughts positive?

David Stevens believed he couldn't fail. He even went to the annual Minnesota Twins tryout camp. The Twins' officials were flabbergasted. They couldn't understand why David was trying out. You see, David had no legs.

The Twins' managers talked to David to find out who he was. They discovered that he was a champion wrestler, he hit .500 on his high school baseball team, and he also played middle guard in football. The Twins asked him, ''Why are you trying out?'' David responded that he didn't have to be to work until 2 p.m., so why not try out? He had no limits or boundaries, did he?

How many of us would never try? We'd think of failing, how we are different, or what other people would say. Don't believe it anymore. With the proper attitude, you can accomplish many things. Like a tiny acorn that can give birth to a mighty oak, you have talent, strengths, and reserve potential. Expect the best in all that you do. Believe in success, not failure. Remember the words of Rev. Jesse Jackson, ''If you can conceive it, if you can believe it, you can achieve it.''

GED READING SAMPLE TEST II (Continued)

GED Reading Passage II: Questions

After reading the passage, answer the following questions. You can look back in the passage for the answers. Shade in the best answer.

a b c d e
0 0 0 0 0

1. Which of the following is the best title for the passage?

    a. Success vs. Failure
    b. Success Stories
    c. Believe You Cannot Fail
    d. Mary and David Succeeded
    e. Your Greatest Resource

a b c d e
0 0 0 0 0

2. According to the passage, a person's success is mostly due to his or her

    a. education
    b. income
    c. attitude
    d. family background
    e. job title

a b c d e
0 0 0 0 0

3. Two positive attitudes worth developing are

    a. Expect the best and believe you can't fail.
    b. Learn to fish and do gymnastics.
    c. Understand how much your body is worth and talk positively.
    d. Try harder and be smarter.
    e. None of the above.

a b c d e
0 0 0 0 0

4. From the passage you can assume that

    a. David Stevens was a failure.
    b. Jesse Jackson thinks people have limited abilities.
    c. People who fish have negative attitudes.
    d. Mary Lou Retton won a gold medal.
    e. Most people are failures.

a b c d e
0 0 0 0 0

5. To be successful, you'll need

    a. Job knowledge
    b. Communication skills
    c. An education
    d. A positive attitude
    e. All of the above

a b c d e
0 0 0 0 0

6. David Stevens had no boundaries because

    a. People felt sorry for him.
    b. He hit .500 in baseball.
    c. He had no legs.
    d. He was lucky.
    e. He believed in himself.

a b c d e
0 0 0 0 0

7. "Your mind will do what it's programmed to do" means

    a. You have to read more.
    b. What you say and think affects what you do.
    c. Shoplifting can go up and down.
    d. You'll fail if you are a shoplifter.
    e. None of the above.

a b c d e
0 0 0 0 0

8. Believing you cannot fail means that

    a. You feel good about yourself in spite of problems.
    b. You'll never make mistakes.
    c. You never lose.
    d. You don't try if you can't be the best.
    e. Success goes with first place.

a b c d e
0 0 0 0 0

9. To expect the best you have to

    a. Get a college degree.
    b. Help others succeed.
    c. Think negatively about your goals.
    d. Think positively about your goals.
    e. Try harder.

a b c d e
0 0 0 0 0

10. Which of the following summarizes the article:

    a. Fishing is boring.
    b. Positive thinking is easy.
    c. Negative thinking will cause you to steal.
    d. Your heart, lungs and brains aren't that valuable.
    e. A positive attitude will increase your success in life.

THE MATH SAMPLE TEST II

Whole numbers

1
$$22 \atop +31$$ 263 +38 **2** 29 −13 931 −69

1
22 +31	263 +38

2
29 −13	931 −69

3
7 ×7	4 ×8	40 ×9	567 ×43

4 4)84   7)4914   37)248   45)1069

Fractions

5
2 1/8 +1 1/8	2 3/7 +1 5/7	5 − 3/4	6 4/5 −5 3/5

6 5 1/3 × 6 2/8   6 × 1/2

7 2 1/6 ÷ 8 1/3   1/2 ÷ 5/8

8 Circle which fraction is largest?

3/7   3/8   11/12   1/2   6/5

Decimals

9
4.21 +6.99	2.91 +11.33

10
13.17 −5.69	$42.36 −16.50

11
.5 ×.5	6.25 ×.61

12 .4).428

13 You work two part-time jobs. On payday one check equaled $125.32 and the other was $79.59. How much money did you receive?

Percent

14 15% of 150 = _____

15 3/4 = _____ %

16 23% of 255 = _____

17 .575 = _____ %

18 If sales tax on clothes is 6% and you purchased $75 in clothing, what does the tax equal? How much would your total bill be?

19 Sally is 25 years old. Her sister Sue is 10 years old. What percent of Sally's age is Sue?

20 Not counting this question, there are 36 problems on this test. If you had 30 correct, what percent correct is that?

ANSWERS TO SAMPLE TEST

Language Sample Test II Answers:
pp. 57–59
1. d
2. c
3. b
4. c
5. d
6. e
7. c
8. a
9. d
10. c
11. e
12. b
13. a
14. a
15. d

GED Reading Passage: Answers
pp. 60–63
1. e
2. c
3. a
4. d
5. e
6. e
7. b
8. a
9. d
10. e

Math Sample Test answers:
pp. 64–65

1. 53	301		
2. 16	862		
3. 49	32	360	24,381
4. 21	702	6r26	23r34
5. 3 1/4	4 1/7	4 1/4	1 1/5
6. 33 1/3	3		
7. 13/50	4/5		
8. 6/5			
9. 11.20	14.24		
10. 7.48	$25.86		
11. .25	3.8125		
12. 1.07			
13. $204.91			
14. 22.5			
15. 75%			
16. 58.65			
17. 57.5%			
18. $4.50	$79.50		
19. 40%			
20. 83.3% correct			

NOTES

FOR OTHER FIFTY-MINUTE SELF-STUDY BOOKS
SEE ORDER FORM AT THE BACK OF THE BOOK.

NOTES

NOTES

NOTES

FOR OTHER FIFTY-MINUTE SELF-STUDY BOOKS
SEE ORDER FORM AT THE BACK OF THE BOOK.

THE FIFTY-MINUTE SERIES

Quantity	Title	Code #	Price	Amount
	MANAGEMENT TRAINING			
	Self-Managing Teams	000-0	$7.95	
	Delegating For Results	008-6	$7.95	
	Successful Negotiation—Revised	09-2	$7.95	
	Increasing Employee Productivity	010-8	$7.95	
	Personal Performance Contracts—Revised	12-2	$7.95	
	Team Building—Revised	16-5	$7.95	
	Effective Meeting Skills	33-5	$7.95	
	An Honest Day's Work: Motivating Employees To Excel	39-4	$7.95	
	Managing Disagreement Constructively	41-6	$7.95	
	Training Managers To Train	43-2	$7.95	
	The Fifty-Minute Supervisor—Revised	58-0	$7.95	
	Leadership Skills For Women	62-9	$7.95	
	Systematic Problem Solving & Decision Making	63-7	$7.95	
	Coaching & Counseling	68-8	$7.95	
	Ethics In Business	69-6	$7.95	
	Understanding Organizational Change	71-8	$7.95	
	Project Management	75-0	$7.95	
	Risk Taking	76-9	$7.95	
	Managing Organizational Change	80-7	$7.95	
	Working Together In A Multi-Cultural Organization	85-8	$7.95	
	Selecting a Consultant	87-4	$7.95	
	PERSONNEL MANAGEMENT			
	Your First Thirty Days: A Professional Image in a New Job	003-5	$7.95	
	Office Management	005-1	$7.95	
	Attacking Absentism	042-6	$7.95	
	Men and Women: Partners at Work	009-4	$7.95	
	Effective Performance Appraisals—Revised	11-4	$7.95	
	Quality Interviewing—Revised	13-0	$7.95	
	Personal Counseling	14-9	$7.95	
	New Employee Orientation	46-7	$7.95	
	Professional Excellence For Secretaries	52-1	$7.95	
	Guide To Affirmative Action	54-8	$7.95	
	Writing A Human Resources Manual	70-X	$7.95	
	Winning at Human Relations	86-6	$7.95	
	WELLNESS			
	Mental Fitness	15-7	$7.95	
	Wellness in the Workplace	020-5	$7.95	
	Personal Wellness	021-3	$7.95	
	Preventing Job Burnout	23-8	$7.95	

THE FIFTY-MINUTE SERIES (Continued)

Quantity	Title	Code #	Price	Amount
	WELLNESS (CONTINUED)			
	Job Performance and Chemical Dependency	27-0	$7.95	
	Overcoming Anxiety	029-9	$7.95	
	Productivity at the Workstation	041-8	$7.95	
	COMMUNICATIONS			
	Technical Writing	004-3	$7.95	
	Giving and Receiving Criticism	023-X	$7.95	
	Effective Presentation Skills	24-6	$7.95	
	Better Business Writing—Revised	25-4	$7.95	
	The Business Of Listening	34-3	$7.95	
	Writing Fitness	35-1	$7.95	
	The Art Of Communicating	45-9	$7.95	
	Technical Presentation Skills	55-6	$7.95	
	Making Humor Work	61-0	$7.95	
	Visual Aids In Business	77-7	$7.95	
	Speed-Reading In Business	78-5	$7.95	
	Publicity Power	82-3	$7.95	
	SELF-MANAGEMENT			
	Attitude: Your Most Priceless Possession-Revised	011-6	$7.95	
	Personal Time Management	22-X	$7.95	
	Successful Self-Management	26-2	$7.95	
	Business Etiquette	032-9	$7.95	
	Balancing Home And Career—Revised	035-3	$7.95	
	Developing Positive Assertiveness	38-6	$7.95	
	Time Management And The Telephone	53-X	$7.95	
	Memory Skills In Business	56-4	$7.95	
	Developing Self-Esteem	66-1	$7.95	
	Creativity In Business	67-X	$7.95	
	Managing Personal Change	74-2	$7.95	
	Stop Procrastinating: Get To Work!	88-2	$7.95	
	CUSTOMER SERVICE/SALES TRAINING			
	Sales Training Basics—Revised	02-5	$7.95	
	Restaurant Server's Guide—Revised	08-4	$7.95	
	Telephone Courtesy And Customer Service	18-1	$7.95	
	Effective Sales Management	031-0	$7.95	
	Professional Selling	42-4	$7.95	
	Customer Satisfaction	57-2	$7.95	
	Telemarketing Basics	60-2	$7.95	
	Calming Upset Customers	65-3	$7.95	
	Quality At Work	72-6	$7.95	
	Managing Quality Customer Service	83-1	$7.95	
	Quality Customer Service—Revised	95-5	$7.95	
	SMALL BUSINESS AND FINANCIAL PLANNING			
	Becoming A Consultant	006-X	$7.95	
	Basic Business Financial Analysis	022-1	$7.95	
	Effective Collection Techniques	034-5	$7.95	
	Marketing Your Consulting Or Professional Services	40-8	$7.95	

THE FIFTY-MINUTE SERIES (Continued)

Quantity	Title	Code #	Price	Amount
	SMALL BUSINESS AND FINANCIAL PLANNING (CONTINUED)			
	Starting Your New Business	44-0	$7.95	
	Personal Financial Fitness—Revised	89-0	$7.95	
	BASIC LEARNING SKILLS			
	Returning To Learning: Getting A G.E.D.	002-7	$7.95	
	Study Skills Strategies—Revised	05-X	$7.95	
	Basic Business Math	024-8	$7.95	
	Becoming An Effective Tutor	028-0	$7.95	
	CAREER PLANNING			
	Career Discovery	07-6	$7.95	
	Networking Your Way to Success	030-2	$7.95	
	Preparing for Your Interview	033-7	$7.95	
	Plan B: Protecting Your Career	48-3	$7.95	
	I Got the Job!	59-9	$7.95	
	RETIREMENT			
	Personal Financial Fitness—Revised	89-0	$7.95	
	Financial Planning	90-4	$7.95	

OTHER CRISP INC. BOOKS

Quantity	Title	Code #	Price	Amount
	Stepping Up To Supervisor	11-8	$13.95	
	The Unfinished Business Of Living: Helping Aging Parents	19-X	$12.95	
	Managing Performance	23-7	$19.95	
	Be True To Your Future: A Guide To Life Planning	47-5	$13.95	
	Up Your Productivity	49-1	$10.95	
	Comfort Zones: Planning Your Future 2/e	73-4	$13.95	
	Copyediting 2/e	94-7	$18.95	
	Practical Time Management	275-4	$13.95	

VIDEO TITLE*

Quantity	Video Title*	Code #	Preview	Purchase	Amount
	Attitude: Your Most Priceless Possession	012-4	$25.00	$395.00	
	Quality Customer Service	013-2	$25.00	$395.00	
	Team Building	014-2	$25.00	$395.00	
	Job Performance & Chemical Dependency	015-9	$25.00	$395.00	
	Better Business Writing	016-7	$25.00	$395.00	
	Creativity in Business	036-1	$25.00	$395.00	
	Honest Day's Work	037-X	$25.00	$395.00	
	Calming Upset Customers	040-X	$25.00	$395.00	
	Balancing Home and Career	048-5	$25.00	$395.00	
	Mental Fitness	049-3	$25.00	$395.00	

(*Note: All tapes are VHS format. Video package includes five books and a Leader's Guide.)

THE FIFTY-MINUTE SERIES
(Continued)

	Amount
Total Books	
Less Discount (5 or more different books 20% sampler)	
Total Videos	
Less Discount (purchase of 3 or more videos earn 20%)	
Shipping ($3.50 per video, $.50 per book)	
California Tax (California residents add 7%)	
TOTAL	

☐ Send volume discount information.

☐ Please charge the following credit card

☐ Please send me a catalog.

☐ Mastercard ☐ VISA ☐ AMEX

Account No. _____ Name (as appears on card) _____

Ship to: _____ Bill to: _____

_____ _____

_____ _____

_____ _____

Phone number: _____ P.O. # _____

All orders except those with a P.O.# must be prepaid.
For more information Call (415) 949-4888 or FAX (415) 949-1610.

NO POSTAGE
NECESSARY
IF MAILED
IN THE
UNITED STATES

BUSINESS REPLY
FIRST CLASS   PERMIT NO. 884   LOS ALTOS, CA

POSTAGE WILL BE PAID BY ADDRESSEE

Crisp Publications, Inc.
95 First Street
Los Altos, CA 94022